on the go

Photography
George Siede and Donna Preis

Louis Weber, C.E.O.
Publications International, Ltd.
7373 North Cicero Avenue
Lincolnwood, Illinois 60646

ISBN 0–7853–1276–5

Publications International, Ltd.

tricycle

wagon

car

truck

fire engine

police car

train

boat

plane

rocket

go, kids